P9-BJN-177

People of Destiny

A Humanities Series

There comes a time,
we know not when,
that marks
the destiny of men.

Joseph Addison Alexander

People of Destiny

HELEN KELLER

By Norman Richards

For his cooperation in reviewing this manuscript the editors wish to express their appreciation to Mr. M. R. Barnett, Executive Director. the American Foundation for the Blind

CHILDRENS PRESS, CHICAGO

The editors wish to express their appreciation to Mr. Meyer Goldberg, who created the series and inspired the publication of People of Destiny.

Cover and body design: John Hollis

Project editor: Joan Downing

Editorial assistant: Gerri Stoller

Illustrations: John Downs—Hollis Associates

Research editor: Robert Hendrickson

Photographs: From the files of Wide World Photos, Inc., Helen Keller Property Board, and Perkins School for the Blind

---

Typesetting: American Typesetting Co.

Printing: The Regenstein Corporation

Quotations on page 16 from The Story of My Life, *by Helen Keller, Doubleday & Company, Inc., 1954.*
Quotations on pages 55, col. 2, ll. 24-30 and 74 from The Three Lives of Helen Keller, *by Richard Harrity and Ralph G. Martin, Doubleday & Company, Inc., 1962.*
Quotations on pages 49; 55, col. 1; 55, col. 2, ll. 35-42; and 63 from Valiant Companions, *by Helen Waite, Macrae Smith Company, 1959.*
Quotation on page 40 from the book Helen Keller: Sketch for a Portrait, *by Van Wyck Brooks. Copyright © 1954, 1956 by Van Wyck Brooks. Reprinted by permission of E. P. Dutton & Co., Inc. and J. M. Dent & Sons, Ltd.*

Library of Congress Catalog Card No. 67-20105
Copyright © 1968 by Regensteiner Publishing Enterprises, Inc. All rights reserved. Printed in the U.S.A. Published simultaneously in Canada.

Contents

A Remarkable Graduate

It was graduation day at Radcliffe College in 1904. Proud parents and friends sat stiffly, the women in their high-necked, starched dresses, the men pulling at their moustaches and fingering their high collars in the warm June air. Ninety-six young women in caps and gowns comprised the graduating class. They represented the cream of American womanhood. Radcliffe had long since earned its reputation as one of the finest women's colleges in the world. These girls had mastered the challenging liberal arts curriculum, considered the most difficult and comprehensive in the country.

College education for women was still something of a rarity in the Victorian era, when they had not yet won the right to vote. America had only lately emerged from a frontier era in the West and it was still a man's country. Women were expected to be wives and mothers at home, or perhaps shopgirls in the industrial East, but the career woman was rare indeed.

Leaders with foresight believed the day would come, however, when skilled, educated women would be needed in our growing country. America was fast emerging as one of the great powers of the world. Only six years before, the young country had won an overwhelming military victory over Spain in a contest that had been watched by the whole world. In manufacturing, mining, agriculture, and transportation, America was leaping ahead of the world with new inventions and efficient methods. Immigrants continued to pour in from Europe, bringing brainpower, ambition, and the ability to work hard.

The Wright brothers had made their historic first flight a year earlier and Henry Ford had begun producing automobiles in Detroit, determined to make a car "for the common man." A young lieutenant named Douglas MacArthur had graduated from West Point with the highest grades ever made and was now on duty in the Philippines, a place where he was to meet his destiny years later. The vigorous Theodore Roosevelt was President of the United States. He gave the country a spirit of youthful enthusiasm.

The speakers at the graduation exercise gave glowing speeches about the promise of the future, and the young women listened intently, the tassels swinging from their caps as they nodded their heads in vigorous agreement. Finally, one by one, they marched up the steps of the platform to receive their coveted degrees.

One graduate did not march up the steps alone. A young woman, not much older than she was, it seemed, walked with her, guiding her. Many of those present knew that this young graduate's name was Helen Keller, and that she was graduating *cum laude*. She was already the author of a best-selling, well-written book about her life, and she had also shown a great ability in languages. These feats alone would have made her a remarkable student, but the facts about her were more than remarkable—they were amazing. Helen Keller could neither speak, nor see, nor hear! None of these abilities were at her command to aid her in studying the complex subjects taught at Radcliffe.

To be sure, she had *begun* to learn to speak, something practically unheard-of for a person who was both deaf and blind. She had "heard" lectures with the aid of her companion-teacher, Anne Sullivan, who had sat with her and transmitted the words and sentences to her by tapping into her hand with a special alphabet. She had learned to touch-type on an ordinary typewriter, the method she had used to communicate with her teachers and do her college work. It would have been impossible to have earned the degree without her selfless companion, Anne Sullivan, who provided the link between ordinary living and Helen Keller's dark and silent world. But the degree would have been equally unattainable had it not been for Helen's intelligence and determination to overcome difficulties greater than most people can imagine.

Newspapers in many parts of the world carried stories about this remarkable young woman. They pointed out that she had brought hope and inspiration to the afflicted in all walks of life. By her very determination and accomplishments she seemed to be saying that it is wrong to give up in despair because of handicaps.

Helen Keller has gone on to live a very prominent life, traveling the world over and devoting the major part of her time to helping the blind and the deaf. She is nearly as well known in foreign countries as she is in her home country, and she is universally admired for her courage and generosity.

It has been Helen Keller's destiny to rise above great obstacles and to electrify the world while doing it. Her life has been filled with personal tragedy, great happiness, and a full range of experiences in between. But two things her life has never lacked are hope and courage.

Helen Keller, the blind, deaf, and mute girl who graduated cum laude *from Radcliffe College in 1904, is shown opposite with her teacher-companion, Anne Sullivan, who sat with Helen and helped her to communicate with her teachers and do her college work. Without Anne, who had provided the link between ordinary living and Helen's dark and silent world, it would have been impossible for Helen to have earned the degree.*

Descent Into Darkness

Helen Keller began life as a pretty child, normal in every way and exceptionally bright. She was born in the small town of Tuscumbia, where the Tennessee River wends its way through the hills of northern Alabama. The area was one of farm fields, trees, and narrow, winding country roads. At the end of one of these roads stood the large, plain Keller house, surrounded by barns, fruit trees, and gardens where vegetables grew.

Her father, Arthur, was a former Confederate army captain and a respected local newspaper editor. A man in his forties, he had been married before and had two sons before he met Kate, his second wife, who was about twenty years younger. They moved into an attractive little cottage on the Keller home grounds, rather than live in the big main house.

When their first child, Helen, was born on June 27, 1880, they were beside themselves with joy. When she was only six months old she uttered her first word, "water," and her parents were surprised that she seemed several months ahead of the learning pace of most babies. She quickly picked up more words and phrases, to the delight of her family and their friends.

Her ability with words was in the tradition of both sides of her family. Not only was her father a good editor, but her mother came from a family that was distinguished in the use of words. She was related to Edward Everett, a famous minister, professor of Greek at Harvard, and orator. He was the principal speaker on the program at Gettysburg on the day Abraham Lincoln gave his Gettysburg Address. He later served as a Congressman, United States Senator, Secretary of State, and president of Harvard University. Another relative of Helen's mother, a cousin, was Edward Everett Hale, clergyman and author of *The Man Without a Country,* a famous book published during the Civil War period.

Helen's parents doted on her and she was always very close to them. Her father was a loving family man who spent as much time as possible with his wife and children—except for the times

Helen Keller was born on June 27, 1880, the first child of Arthur and Kate Keller. The family lived in Tuscumbia, Alabama, in an attractive cottage on the Keller home grounds, rather than live in Ivy Green, the big main house shown at the top of page thirteen. The room in which Helen was born is shown at the bottom of page thirteen. At the foot of the four-poster bed is the cradle in which she slept during the first few months of her life.

he went hunting with his friends. He loved his family homestead with its turkeys, chickens, pigs, and sheep and its ivy-covered fences and buildings. The air was clean and sweet with the aroma of wild flowers and ripening fruit blossoms. It was a peaceful, unhurried life.

Helen Keller enjoyed nineteen months of this secure, happy existence before it was cruelly taken away from her. One cold day in February the bright, lively little tot developed a fever. Her father sent for a doctor, who examined her but could find no symptoms of disease. He prescribed a fever-reducing medicine and told the Kellers they would have to wait and see what developed.

Helen's fever persisted in spite of the medicine. She was a very sick child. Her eyes were inflamed and light seemed to bother her.

The doctor visited her again a few days later and seemed very worried.

"This girl is very sick," he said. "I'm afraid she has an acute form of congestion of the stomach . . . and the brain."

"Will she live, doctor?" Mr. and Mrs. Keller asked together. They held their breath.

"She is in real danger and I can't say," the doctor replied. "But she's strong and that may pull her through."

For the next several days Mrs. Keller sat by Helen's bed hour after hour, trying to comfort the child. She refused to leave except to catch a quick nap now and then. She prayed silently for Helen's life to be spared.

It seemed as if her prayers were finally answered when one morning Helen's fever disappeared. The fitful youngster fell into a peaceful sleep and later that day, after the doctor had examined her, he told her parents not to worry any more. She would be bouncing around again in a few days, he predicted.

Then came the tragic shock.

A couple of days later Helen's mother spoke to her as she lay in bed and wondered why she didn't reply. She spoke again, but still there was no reply. She noticed that the girl stared fixedly at the ceiling with no expression.

Suddenly Mrs. Keller had a terrible thought.

"Don't you see me, Helen?" she asked.

She asked it again, in a voice rising with fear. She tried to make the girl blink by passing her hand over her face and by clapping. There was no response at all.

Mrs. Keller was terrified and she ran to get her husband. By the time she brought him to the room she was sobbing hysterically.

"She can't see us or hear us!" she cried.

"It can't be true!" Mr. Keller exclaimed. "Here, let me see," he said, bending over the girl's bed and looking into her expressionless eyes.

He tried waving a hand over her eyes, but her eyelids didn't move.

"Don't you see us, Helen?" he begged. "Please tell me." He was almost in tears. "Please. Please."

"It won't do any good to talk to her," Mrs. Keller sobbed. "She can't hear us at all."

"Oh God, she's alone in the dark!" Mr. Keller whispered in despair.

The Kellers refused to accept the permanence of Helen's tragedy. They took her to eye and ear specialists and had her examined. They asked if there were any possibility of either her sight or hearing being restored through oper-

Helen was a bright baby who began to speak at a very early age. Her parents cared very much for her and for nineteen months she enjoyed a secure and happy existence. Then she developed a fever that persisted for days. A day or two after the fever broke and Helen appeared to be recovering, her parents made a tragic discovery (opposite). The child could neither see nor hear them.

ations. Over and over again they were told no, but they kept going to other doctors and trying again. It was no use.

"Gradually I got used to the silence and darkness that surrounded me and forgot that it had ever been any different," Helen Keller wrote years later.

The loneliness must have been overwhelming to the little girl, but Helen eventually began taking an interest in things around her. She followed her mother closely around the house, hanging onto her skirt. Her natural curiosity and intelligence caused her to explore as best she could.

"My hands felt every object and observed every motion," she wrote, "and in this way I learned to know many things. . . . A shake of the head meant 'No' and a nod 'Yes,' a pull meant 'Come' and a push 'Go.' . . . I would imitate the acts of cutting the slices (for bread) and buttering them. . . . If I wanted ice cream . . . I made the sign for working the freezer and shivered, indicating cold. My mother . . . succeeded in making me understand a good deal. . . . Indeed, I owe to her loving wisdom all that was bright and good in my long night."

By the time Helen was several years old, she realized that she was different from other people. She would feel people's faces as she did everything else, and she noticed that their lips moved when they wanted something done, rather than their hands. At times she would stand between two people who were talking and touch their lips. She felt so frustrated at not being able to understand that she would have fits of temper. She sometimes kicked and

screamed in anger. By this time she had forgotten the words she had been able to speak before her illness, because she had not heard them since. Thus, she was dumb as well as deaf and blind, and could make only animal sounds.

Her frustration increased as she grew older and found that signs and motions did not explain all the things she was curious about. Her lively, intelligent mind wanted to comprehend more than the simple messages transmitted to her. As a result of her frustration she grew bad-tempered and impatient.

After a temper tantrum she would often run into the garden and wander about, sniffing the flowers and playing by herself. She loved flowers and could tell the different kinds by their scents. She seemed happier in the garden than anywhere else.

Helen was fortunate to have as a playmate Martha Washington, the little daughter of the Keller family cook. Martha quickly learned to understand Helen's signs and motions. They played together constantly in the fields and woods and even helped milk the cows and did chores in the kitchen. They got into quite a bit of mischief, too. They once stole a freshly baked cake and ran behind a woodpile to eat the whole thing. Another time they cut each other's hair with scissors, and once Helen locked her mother in the pantry for three hours and laughed gleefully about it.

Helen was five years old when the family moved from the little cottage to the larger main house on the homestead. Not long afterward a little sister, Mildred, was born. Helen's parents had spoiled her since her illness and they believed they should let her go unpunished for most of her mischief and tantrums because of her handicaps. She was used to being the center of attention and it didn't take her long to become jealous of the new baby. It seemed to her that every time she would begin to crawl into her mother's lap, the newcomer was already there.

To add insult to injury, one morning Helen found the baby asleep in her own doll's cradle that she loved to rock. She ran to the cradle and angrily knocked it over. The baby flew into the air and could have been badly hurt if Mrs. Keller hadn't come into the room at that instant and caught her. When she gave Helen a little slap to let her know she was angry, Helen became enraged. She ran around the room, kicking and making animal sounds and knocking things over.

This sort of behavior became more and more frequent as the months went by. Helen's parents continued to let her have her own way in almost everything, and she had few guidelines for behavior. But the strain was becoming obvious for all members of the family.

They had not succeeded in teaching Helen any manners and this proved embarrassing, particularly at the dinner table. Helen grabbed her food and stuffed it into her mouth with her hands, like an animal. She often ran around the table, snatching food from other people's dishes and sometimes throwing it on the floor. Most of the time her parents didn't protest this behavior, but when they did, Helen always flew into a tantrum.

Mr. and Mrs. Keller began to wonder just what they could do to solve the baffling problem of communicating with their daughter and helping her to learn better behavior. The time had come, they decided, when they had to obtain help from professionals.

Though the loneliness must have been overwhelming for the little girl in her dark and silent world, Helen eventually began taking an interest in things around her. It was frustrating for her not to be able to understand what people were saying and doing, and she often had temper tantrums. When she was five years old, the family moved into the big main house, and not long afterward a sister, Mildred, was born. Suddenly, Helen was no longer the center of attention and she became jealous of the new baby. One morning, Helen found her sister in the doll's cradle and she became so angry that she knocked it over (left). The baby flew into the air and could have been badly hurt if Mrs. Keller hadn't come into the room at that instant and caught her.

A Helper for the Blind

Many specialists had told the Kellers that it would be impossible to restore Helen's sight and hearing, but their love and hope for their daughter made them try again. This time, when Helen was about five, they took her on a long train trip to Baltimore to see a prominent oculist named Chisholm. But once again the verdict was the same: Helen would never see.

In despair Mr. Keller said, "Helen will never be able to do anything in this world."

"That's not true," replied the doctor. "I think this child can be educated. I don't think she should have to lead a useless life because she's blind and deaf."

Dr. Chisholm suggested that the Kellers take Helen to Dr. Alexander Graham Bell, the prominent Scottish-born teacher of the deaf and inventor of the telephone. Dr. Bell had followed in the footsteps of his father, a leader in teaching speech and helping the deaf.

It was while he experimented with systems to record visibly the vibrations of the voice that Dr. Bell had discovered a method of transmitting speech over an electric wire—the telephone.

His main career, however, had always been teaching the deaf. He had opened a school for the deaf in Boston and had been a professor of vocal physiology at Boston University. His methods were invaluable and are still basic in teaching the deaf.

"If anybody in this world can tell you whether Helen can be taught to communicate, he can," Dr. Chisholm had said.

It didn't take Alexander Graham Bell long to determine that Helen was indeed intelligent and had the desire to learn. He held the child on his knee and struck an immediate rapport with her. He was a gentle, fatherly man who genuinely loved children, and Helen seemed to sense this.

Helen's behavior became worse as the months went by, and her parents soon realized that they needed professional help in learning how to communicate with their daughter. Many specialists had told the Kellers that it would be impossible to restore Helen's sight and hearing, but a doctor in Baltimore told them he thought Helen could be educated. He sent them to see Dr. Alexander Graham Bell, the Scottish-born teacher of the deaf and inventor of the telephone. It didn't take this man long to determine that Helen was indeed intelligent and had the desire to learn. He held the child on his knee (opposite) and played several games with her as he watched her reactions.

Dr. Bell advised the Kellers to contact the Perkins Institution for the Blind in Boston. The director of the school, Michael Anagnos, would be able to find a teacher for Helen. A teacher in a Paris school, Louis Braille (opposite), had invented a system of raised letters that people who were blind could read by touching them with their fingers. That system, along with the patience and knowledge of the teachers at the Perkins School, would be invaluable in teaching Helen how to understand and communicate with others.

Dr. Bell took his large, round watch from his pocket and put it in Helen's hand. Then he pressed a button on it and it chimed. Helen could feel the vibrations of the chimes, and she quickly discovered that she could make the watch chime again by pressing the button. She laughed in delight and pressed the button again and again.

Dr. Bell played several games with her, all the while watching her reactions. Finally he turned to her parents.

"This little girl is intelligent and she wants to learn everything she can," he said. "The reason you can't teach her normal behavior is that you are unable to communicate enough with her. And she feels frustrated and angry because she can't learn more."

Dr. Bell told the Kellers that it would be a long, difficult struggle, but that the right teacher would be able to get through to Helen. It would require a person with great patience and complete understanding of the problems of the blind and deaf.

He advised them to contact the Perkins Institution for the Blind, a noted training establishment in Boston and the first school in America to teach the blind. Michael Anagnos, the Greek-born director of the school, would be the person best qualified to find a teacher for Helen, Dr. Bell said.

At this point in history—1886—training for the blind had been progressing for many years, thanks to the efforts of leaders who were as dedicated to helping the sightless as Alexander Graham Bell was to helping the deaf.

The first real organized efforts to educate the blind had taken place in France near the end of the eighteenth century. Valentin Haüy, who later came to be known as the "Father and Apostle of the Blind," had met a blind boy, François Lesueur, who was begging in the streets of Paris. Impressed with the boy's alertness, he offered to educate him and pay for his living expenses. He soon discovered a method of embossing raised letters that the youngster could decipher.

Haüy soon had a dozen pupils, and in 1784 officially opened the *Institute Nationale des Jeunes Aveugles.* Schools patterned after his efforts were opened in Great Britain, Russia, Germany, and Sweden, and by 1830 there were three schools for the blind in the United States.

One of the teachers in the Paris school was Louis Braille, who invented an effective system of reading that came to be known as braille. Although embossed letters for the blind had been used before, Braille's system was so much better that it came to be preferred, and still is today.

The system made use of groups of dots, with a maximum of six in each group. The groups, depending on the

number and position of dots in each one, represent the letters of the alphabet, numbers, and punctuation signs. With this system a blind person can learn to read without depending on his hearing alone for communication. Braille can also be written with a special slate and a stylus for punching out the raised dots.

Thanks to these and other pioneers, blind people had an opportunity in the nineteenth century to learn the skills of communication. The deaf, too, could be taught the hand alphabet and to read lips. But those rare people with the triple handicap of being blind, deaf, and dumb had been beyond help until a great development occurred at the Perkins Institution for the Blind.

Dr. Samuel Gridley Howe, head of the school, was not only a great teacher but also a romantic idealist who refused to believe that the impossible could not be made possible. He had taken part in a revolution in Greece and had written a history of it; he then took part in a Polish revolution because of his fervent belief in helping people fight for freedom. His wife, Julia Ward Howe, wrote the "Battle Hymn of the Republic," the famous song that inspired soldiers during the American Civil War.

Dr. Howe began trying to teach blind children at his father's house in Boston while he was still a young man. As he accepted more and more pupils, he moved his quarters to a larger building in Boston. It was named the Perkins Institution.

In 1837 Dr. Howe admitted his most challenging pupil to the school—Laura Bridgman. She was an eight-year-old child who had been stricken with scarlet fever at the age of twenty-six months. The disease had left her blind, deaf, and dumb, and had also taken away her sense of smell and taste. She was completely isolated from the world, and Dr. Howe wanted to find a way to enable her to communicate.

He began by using raised braille-type letters and pasting them on objects such as forks, spoons, knives, and keys. After awhile she associated these objects with the letters on them. The next step was to teach her that combinations of letters could spell other words, too. After she had learned this, he had one of his teachers learn the manual alphabet from a deaf-mute and teach it to Laura. This is a method of tapping on a person's hand, with each combination of taps meaning a different letter.

Dr. Samuel Gridley Howe, director of the Perkins School before Michael Anagnos, had figured out a way to teach Laura Bridgman (opposite), a blind, deaf, and mute girl, how to communicate. Though as a child she was completely isolated from the world, Dr. Howe and his teachers were able to teach her language. Laura stayed at Perkins for the rest of her life, learning to crochet, sew, and communicate with the other people at the institution.

Dr. Howe and his teachers were soon teaching Laura language, and she was able to express herself well with the manual alphabet. She remained at Perkins for the rest of her life, learning to crochet, sew, and communicate with the other people at the institution. This was an historic achievement, for no blind, deaf-mute had ever been able to communicate this well before.

The famous British novelist, Charles Dickens, had written a fine article about Laura and her teacher in his book *American Notes* after a visit to the United States. Helen Keller's mother had read his book years later and remembered what Dr. Howe had been able to accomplish with Laura Bridgman. Dr. Howe had since died, but the Perkins Institution was carrying on his work. Dr. Howe's scientific records of Laura's progress were considered valuable to future teachers of the blind and deaf.

The Kellers wrote to Michael Anagnos, now directing the school, and told him of Dr. Alexander Graham Bell's advice to let him find the best teacher for Helen. They waited and waited for a reply, growing more anxious every day. Several weeks went by.

Then one morning Mr. Keller walked out to the mailbox beside the road and found a letter from Michael Anagnos. He tore the envelope open and scanned the letter.

He ran into the house shouting that a teacher had been found who would help Helen! Mrs. Keller fairly trembled with joy.

"Anne Sullivan is her name, but it doesn't say much about her background," Mr. Keller said.

They couldn't have guessed how unhappy Anne Sullivan's background had been. She was only twenty, but her life had been one of misery and struggle. She had been born in Massachusetts in 1866, the year after the Civil War ended. She was the daughter of Irish immigrants, and at this point in history thousands of Irish were pouring into Massachusetts as an aftermath of the potato famine and the terrible conditions in their home country. They held the lowest-paying jobs in Massachusetts and were looked down upon, for the most part, as ignorant peasants.

Anne's father never succeeded in rising above the poverty he lived in, and her mother died when she was only eight years old. Two years after her death, Anne's father abandoned his three children and Anne was placed in a state home. It was a terrible institution for the poor, and many of the inmates died of disease and malnutrition. Day after day a wagon came and hauled away corpses.

Anne had always had trouble with her eyes, and she became almost totally blind while at the poorhouse. She had

---

The Kellers waited several weeks for a reply to their letter to Michael Anagnos. Then one morning when Mr. Keller went out to the mailbox beside the road, he found a letter from the school (opposite). Mr. Anagnos had found a teacher for Helen.

US
MAIL

no friends or relatives to visit her, and her lonely life was shared only by the pitiful inmates of the institution. She wanted desperately to leave this wretched place. Other inmates told her that there were schools for the blind, and she wished she could enter one.

Her big opportunity came after four years in the institution. The place's reputation was so bad that the state finally sent a committee of investigators. Anne asked these gentlemen if she could go to a school for the blind and they arranged it for her.

In October of 1880, when she was fourteen, Anne entered the Perkins Institution. It was the first place where she was treated kindly—a strange experience for this lonely girl. She was taught to read with her fingers, as all the blind students were, and began receiving an education in many subjects. She had several partially successful operations on both eyes at a Boston hospital, and soon she could see fairly well and could read ordinary print.

Anne was determined to overcome any obstacles, and she was a good student. She learned the deaf-mute's manual alphabet and became friendly with Laura Bridgman, who was now a grown woman living at Perkins. After six years, Anne Sullivan was graduated as valedictorian of her class. She was ready to go out into the world, handicaps and all. She didn't have the best formal education and her eyesight was not good enough for some jobs. Yet she felt there might be some way she could use her education and experience with deaf and blind people.

The opportunity came when Michael Anagnos needed a teacher with the right qualifications for Helen Keller. He knew he could find teachers with more formal education than Anne Sullivan had had, but he doubted that he could find one with more understanding of a blind person's problems, nor one with more patience and determination. She could read braille, knew the manual alphabet, and had known Laura Bridgman well. She had seen the educational methods of Perkins Institution at work and understood them.

Anne accepted the job immediately, but not without some misgivings. It meant moving to a strange place and living with strange people. And she wondered whether she would succeed in teaching this blind deaf-mute without the experts of Perkins nearby to advise her. But up to then she had faced too many difficulties in life to be afraid of any obstacles, and she resolutely packed her bags.

Anne Sullivan (opposite), the teacher Michael Anagnos was sending for Helen, had had a miserable childhood, most of which had been spent in a terrible institution for the poor. Anne, who had become almost blind during her four years there, was fortunate enough to be sent to the Perkins School. There she was educated and was given medical help for her poor eyesight.

Tuscumbia

Teacher's Task

A hoarse toot of the engine whistle announced to the little town of Tuscumbia, Alabama, that a passenger train was puffing down the track. It was 6:30 p.m. on March 3, 1887. A small group of people were gathered at the depot to watch the arrival of the train. Mustachioed and bewhiskered gentlemen stepped briskly off the train, and women clung to their bonnets and lifted the hems of their long skirts as they stepped down.

At last a weary young woman got off, dressed in heavy woolens more appropriate for chilly Boston weather than for this mild Alabama evening. She looked around a bit apprehensively before Mrs. Keller caught her eye.

"Are you Anne Sullivan?" she asked.

"Yes, Mrs. Keller," Anne answered, pleased to find her such a young and pleasant woman. While Mr. Keller's son James picked up Anne's bags, the two women talked on the way to the waiting carriage.

Mrs. Keller, too, was surprised to find Anne so young. In fact, she was a bit worried about whether such a young girl would be able to handle a difficult youngster like Helen.

"Helen was so wild today that we had to leave her at home," she said. "I'm afraid you have a very difficult task ahead of you, and I hope you won't get discouraged too soon," she added.

On March 3, 1887, a small group of people were gathered at the train depot in Tuscumbia, Alabama (opposite), awaiting the arrival of the evening train. Among those who waited were Mr. and Mrs. Keller, for this was the train that would bring Anne Sullivan to their daughter Helen.

What a pleasant place, thought Anne, as the carriage jogged along the dirt road toward the Keller home. Spring came sooner here than in New England, and fruit trees already were in blossom. The grass was green and the freshly ploughed fields gave a rich, earthy aroma in the warm spring evening. Crickets and grasshoppers sang in the meadows.

The carriage rumbled into the Keller driveway, past the gate and up to the house. Mr. Keller came out to meet them and welcomed Anne warmly. The introduction had hardly been completed when Anne asked to meet Helen.

"She's over there on the steps," Mr. Keller said, nodding toward six-year-old Helen. Anne had expected to see a pale, slender, nervous girl such as the children she had known in her own childhood. She was surprised to find that Helen was plump, sturdy, and glowing with health. Good food, sunshine, and the exercise of playing outdoors had made her very strong.

Anne quickly found out how wild and unmanageable Helen was when the youngster grabbed at her handbag and tried to open it. When Mrs. Keller stopped her, she threw a temper tantrum, kicking and screaming. Anne finally placated her by letting her hold her watch, and the girl quieted down.

The next day Helen came up to Anne's room as she was unpacking her bags and hanging her clothes in the closet. She quickly delved into the bags, curious to see what Anne had. Suddenly her hands came up with a doll. She pointed to the doll, then to herself, trying to ask if the doll was for her. Anne put the child's hand on her own head and nodded yes, then pointed to Helen. Helen's face glowed with happiness and she held the doll in both arms.

Anne decided that this would be a good chance to try to teach Helen her first word in the manual alphabet. Taking the child's hand, she spelled D-O-L-L on her palm. At first Helen did not understand, but she was curious. Anne repeated the spelling several times.

Then she made the mistake of taking the doll out of Helen's arms to show her the alphabet better. Helen kicked, hit, and screamed. Anne was kicked in the shins but finally wrestled Helen to a chair and held her there, out of breath.

Then she got an idea. She let Helen go and went down to the kitchen to get a piece of cake. Helen was still sitting sullenly in the room when she returned with the cake. Holding it near the youngster's face so she could smell it, Anne waited for the reaction. Helen loved cake and quickly grabbed for it. But Anne took it away even more quickly. Then she took the child's hand and spelled C-A-K-E into her palm, twice. Helen's intelligent mind grasped the association, and she spelled the word into Anne's palm. Anne delightedly rewarded her with the piece of cake, and she wolfed it down.

Now Anne followed up by presenting the doll for a moment and then spelling D-O-L-L into her hand again. This time Helen understood perfectly and spelled the word without hesitation. Anne quickly gave her the doll to keep. Helen ran downstairs, showed the doll to her mother and even spelled the word into her hand. Her mother didn't understand the manual alphabet, of course, and asked Anne what the child was trying to do. When Anne told her, she was amazed to think that Helen knew what words were.

"She doesn't, yet," Anne answered. "She knows these signs mean something, but she doesn't realize that the individual letters combine to make words. But someday she will understand that, and then I will be able to teach her language, so she can express herself in words."

Helen continued to learn to spell out words in Anne's hand, and Anne was pleased to find that she was an intelligent child. She realized, however, that Helen would not be able to adjust to being with other people until she learned what it meant to behave properly. She continued to act like an animal much of the time.

Mr. and Mrs. Keller continued their way of spoiling Helen and not making her learn manners, and this discouraged Anne. She realized that the time was coming when she would have to start teaching Helen some discipline.

It came soon, at the breakfast table. Helen was behaving as she usually did, grabbing her food with her hands and running around the table, snatching food from other people. As usual, her parents did nothing to stop her. But Anne did.

As Helen tried to grab food from Anne's plate, Anne stopped her and pushed her away. Then she sat Helen down in her chair. Helen leaped up again, but Anne seized her wrists and tried to make her sit down again. Helen screamed and kicked at her, then stamped on the floor.

"Leave her alone, Miss Sullivan," said Mr. Keller, "it creates too much noise at the breakfast table."

Anne was shocked. "Can't you see that she's *got* to learn to act like a human being instead of an animal?" she asked. "Please let me teach her some manners."

Mr. Keller scowled. He didn't like being talked to this way.

Mrs. Keller tried to calm things and said, "Why don't you let her have her way just this once, Anne?"

But Anne was adamant. "No—that's the trouble," she said. "Everybody gives her her way and she'll never learn obedience until this situation stops. I'm not being cruel to her by making her learn manners. I'm being kind, for in the long run she will be a happier person by getting along with other people."

Then Anne asked the Kellers to please leave the room and let her deal with Helen alone. They objected at first, but finally agreed to let her try to do things her way. They slowly walked out of the room and closed the door.

Anne quickly locked it so Helen couldn't run away, then sat down and ate her breakfast without paying any attention to Helen. The savage little youngster kicked, screamed, and rolled on the floor for half an hour, but Anne paid no attention. Helen ran around the table and found that the others had gone, so she sat down and began to eat her own breakfast—but with her hands.

Anne handed her a spoon and indicated that she should eat with it, but Helen threw it on the floor. Anne pulled her out of her chair and tried to make her pick it up. Helen fought violently, kicking and knocking half the dishes off the table, and they struggled on the floor for almost another half hour. Anne won, and she made the wild youngster pick up the spoon and sit in her chair. Then she forced her to eat with it. Helen finally gave up and ate with it herself.

But Helen wasn't tamed yet. When she had finished eating, Anne indicated that she should fold her napkin and leave it on the table. Instead, Helen threw it on the floor. Anne struggled to force her to pick it up and fold it, and

---

Anne quickly discovered that Helen had been spoiled by her family and was completely untrained. Anne would have to teach her how to behave before she could go on to teach her how to communicate. When Helen behaved wildly at the breakfast table (opposite), Anne took the opportunity to begin her first lesson in discipline. After persuading the rest of the family to leave the room, she spent two hours forcing Helen to understand that she must eat her breakfast properly. Anne won her point, but this was only the first of many exhausting episodes with Helen.

Helen kicked and screamed for nearly another hour. They wrestled and wrestled until finally Helen gave in and folded the napkin. At last Anne let Helen go out into the garden and sighed heavily. Then she dragged herself upstairs to her room, lay down on her bed and cried.

She had won an important point, but she knew that part of Helen's trouble was the sympathetic attitude of her parents toward her bad behavior. She could never change the child's wild ways as long as her parents were there to comfort her.

The next day Anne asked for permission to move into the little cottage where the family had lived during Helen's first five years. She and Helen would live there, and the parents could look in occasionally to see how they were doing. Mr. and Mrs. Keller reluctantly agreed, but only after much pleading by Anne for a chance to teach Helen in her own way.

The first few days were filled with Helen's tantrums and more struggling, but each time she was made to give in and obey. Within a few days she began behaving very well, when she saw it did no good to act wildly. Then Anne began to teach her more and more words. She tried to teach Helen to spell words instead of just the things she wanted. She hoped that someday there would be a "breakthrough"—that Helen would know that letters form words and that words have meanings. Then she would be able to put sentences together and express her thoughts. Without this ability she had no contact with the world except for simple signs to show what she wanted. Years later, Helen wrote that during this period of her life she was like a ship groping its way through dense fog, and that life had little meaning for her.

Anne pushed doggedly on, teaching Helen to knit, to crochet, and to sew in just a few days. Helen's intelligence and natural curiosity delighted Anne, and she knew that some day Helen would understand what words were for. That day was to come sooner than she expected.

The Kellers had become used to letting Helen have her own way most of the time and couldn't help thinking that Anne was too hard on her. Anne knew that it would be very difficult for her to work with Helen as long as they were present, and therefore asked permission to move into the little cottage where the family had lived during Helen's first five years (opposite). She and Helen would live there and the parents could look in occasionally to see how they were doing. Mr. and Mrs. Keller reluctantly agreed, but only after much pleading by Anne for a chance to teach Helen in her own way.

Miracle in Alabama

Like a wild animal, Helen had shunned affection, but after only two weeks in the cottage she began to show that she liked Anne. Before long Mr. and Mrs. Keller missed her so much, though, that they asked Anne to move back into the main house with the youngster. By now Anne felt that it could be done, since Helen had learned to mind. And, with only one or two lapses, this proved to be true.

Anne had been with the Kellers only a month when the magic day of the "breakthrough" arrived. It was a lovely April morning and Anne and Helen were operating the outdoor hand water pump while Helen washed her face and hands. Anne again took the occasion to try to teach Helen the meanings of words, as she had been doing day after day.

She had been trying to make the girl understand the difference between the words "water" and "mug," but without success. The family cook's little boy was pumping water into a bucket, and while he was doing this, Anne made Helen hold a mug under the spout with one hand. As the water spilled into the mug and over Helen's hand, Anne spelled W-A-T-E-R into her other hand.

Suddenly Helen dropped the mug and stood with the cold water rushing over her hand, as though she were in a trance. All at once a radiant look came over her face, and it was clear that she knew that the letters W-A-T-E-R spelled a word, and that word was the name for the cold liquid splashing over her hand.

Helen took Anne's hand and spelled out W-A-T-E-R several times in a row.

After two weeks in the cottage, Helen had learned to mind and had begun to show that she liked Anne. The Kellers, by this time, missed their daughter too much to leave her at the cottage any longer, and Anne agreed to move back into the main house with Helen. Only two weeks later the magic day of the "breakthrough" arrived. Anne and Helen were operating the outdoor water pump (opposite) while Helen washed her face and hands. Anne had been trying to teach Helen the difference between the words "water" and "mug," but without success. Suddenly a radiant look came over Helen's face and it was clear that she knew that the letters w-a-t-e-r spelled the name for the cold liquid splashing over her hand. From that day on, Helen understood that everything has a name and that she would be able to learn to communicate with other people.

If this cold liquid had a name, everything else must, too. What was the name of the ground? She quickly bent down and asked Anne by motioning. Anne spelled it into her hand. Then, growing more excited, she pointed to the pump and the trellis, and finally to Anne herself. To the last question, Anne spelled T-E-A-C-H-E-R.

Neither teacher nor pupil could contain her joy, and they raced back to the main house. All the way back Helen touched every object she could and Anne spelled its name to her. Anne almost shouted the news to Mrs. Keller, who could hardly believe it. Then she rushed up to her room to write the good news to the people at Perkins Institution.

For the rest of the day Helen ran around in a state of excitement, thrilled with the discovery that words had meanings. She pointed to every object she could find and Anne spelled the meaning. Soon she understood verbs like "walk," "sit," and "run," as well as nouns.

Years later Helen wrote, "there was a strange stir within me—a misty consciousness, a sense of something remembered. It was as if I had come back to life after being dead. . . . I understood that it was possible for me to communicate with other people by these signs. Thoughts that ran forward and backward came to me quickly—thoughts that seemed to start in my brain and spread all over me. I think it was in the nature of a revelation. . . . I felt joyous, strong, equal to my limitations. Delicious sensations rippled through me, and sweet strange things that were locked up in my heart began to sing."

The joy in the eyes of Helen's parents touched Anne deeply. When it came time to say good night, Mr. Keller squeezed Anne's hand and started to say something, but his voice was choked with emotion and he couldn't say it. Anne's eyes brimmed with tears of happiness as she mounted the stairs to the room in which she now slept with Helen.

As she slipped under the covers, Helen cuddled close to her and kissed her for the first time since she had met her. It was the most triumphant day of Anne Sullivan's young life.

Now that the dam had burst, there was no stopping the flow of questions from Helen nor her desire to learn everything. She not only learned many new words in the next few weeks, but figured out how to combine them in simple sentences. Soon Anne could give her commands such as "go downstairs and get some bread." Helen understood the sentence perfectly.

Anne decided that the next step was to teach Helen how to read. This task is usually difficult and time-consuming with a child of normal sight and hearing, but with Helen it could be much more difficult.

But once again, Helen's extraordinary intelligence helped her to overcome the obstacles and learn rapidly. The first thing Anne did was teach her the alphabet in raised letters. She already knew the alphabet in sign language, of course, but now she learned it as it is seen on a printed page. She traced the outlines of the letters with her finger, and learned all of them, both capital and small, in one day.

Anne managed to buy some simple storybooks in raised print and put these to immediate use. To teach Helen to recognize words in print, she invented a game. She knew that Helen's lively mind thrived on competition and games, and that this would be the best way to teach her. In this particular game, Anne would name a word and both of them would try to find it in one of the books. The one who found the word first was the winner. After Anne deliberately won the first couple of tries, Helen was spurred on to beat her, and she soon was doing very well.

Once Helen had mastered the raised alphabet, Anne lost no time in launching her on the next project—to learn braille. This system of raised dots presented no baffling challenge to Helen and soon she could read it quite well.

Anne was amazed and delighted that the young girl could absorb knowledge so fast. Anne continued to plunge on, teaching Helen another step as soon as

Once Helen had learned that words have meanings, there was no stopping the flow of questions from her nor her desire to learn everything. She not only learned many new words very quickly, but also figured out how to form sentences. From there she learned the raised alphabet and immediately went on to learn braille. At right is a page of this book typed in braille.

Helen Keller had a lively imagination, and Anne realized that for her learning was fun and a daily part of life. She tried to keep it a game for Helen, and took her for long walks in the country, answering her eager questions as they walked. Helen hardly realized she was learning. Anne and the Kellers took Helen to the circus one day (opposite), where she had a wonderful opportunity to learn about the jungle animals.

she had mastered the previous one. One day she decided it was time to teach Helen to write.

Blind people can be taught to write a special square printing style that can be read by people with sight. This is a wonderful advantage to them, for they can write letters to people who have no knowledge of braille. They learn with a special writing frame with grooves; by feeling the grooves, they can write straight lines.

Anne drilled her over and over, forcing her to repeat her writing until it became clearly readable. It was not easy, but the practice paid off and eventually Helen could write quite well.

Without pausing, Anne now began to teach Helen to write braille as well as read it. Writing braille is difficult, and must be done with a stylus by punching the dots from the underside of the paper. This means that the letters must be punched right to left, so that they will read left to right on the opposite side of the paper. Not only did Helen master this form of writing, but she began to learn braille arithmetic as well.

Once she had learned the basic braille, Mr. Keller bought her a braille writing machine. This type of machine has keys like a typewriter with the raised braille letters on them. When the keys are struck, dots are punched on the underside of the paper and words can be read immediately when the paper is taken

out of the machine. This was more fun to Helen than the pencil-writing lessons, for she could read what she had written in braille, but not in the other form of writing.

Incredibly, Helen had now mastered four different alphabets: the manual one for the deaf, the square pencil script, raised letters, and braille dots. And she was still only seven years old!

For a child with Helen's lively imagination, strict, scheduled lessons might have been too confining and discouraging. But Anne had enough imagination herself to realize that to Helen learning was fun and a daily part of life. She tried to keep it a game for her, and she wisely didn't insist on rigid schedules for lessons. She knew that Helen loved flowers, trees, grass, and nature in general, for instance, and she took her for long walks in the country, answering her eager questions as they walked. She was able to teach the girl proper use of words while answering her, and Helen hardly realized she was learning, because she was having such fun.

Anne and the Kellers took Helen to the circus one day, and she had a wonderful opportunity to learn about the jungle animals there. The performers had been told that Helen was deaf and blind, and they made things interesting for her. She was allowed to feed the elephants and monkeys, ride on an elephant, and fondle young lion cubs.

The first Christmas after Anne's arrival was also the first Helen could understand. Anne told her what Christmas was and she took her shopping to buy presents for Mr. and Mrs. Keller. She also took Helen to a local school Christmas party and she had an enjoyable time with the other children. She hung her stocking by the fireplace on Christmas Eve for the first time, with great hopes that Santa Claus would fill it. The next morning, like millions of other children, she was delighted to find presents and treats in it. At last she was able to share in the joy of Christmas.

Anne continued to write enthusiastic letters to Perkins Institution about Helen's remarkable progress, and Michael Anagnos was especially delighted. As time went on, Anne took Helen and Mrs. Keller on a visit to Perkins, which Helen enjoyed immensely. She met many of the other children in the school, and was delighted to find that they knew the manual alphabet and could "talk" with her with their hands. In fact, they were as adept at using it as she was, and she was able to talk as rapidly as she wanted to. She felt very much at ease among them.

The time finally came when Anne realized that Helen was learning with such ability that she did not have the proper books and facilities to teach her as well as would be necessary in the future. Michael Anagnos offered to take Helen in as a student at no charge, with Anne to continue teaching her by her own methods, but within the school.

Mr. and Mrs. Keller hated to see their little girl go so far from home, but they agreed to accept the offer. The miracles that Anne had wrought with her teaching foretold even more progress for the future. So Helen Keller took her first big step away from home.

The photograph at right was taken when Helen Keller was twelve years old. By this time she had been taken on a visit to the Perkins Institution for the Blind and had met many of the children in the school. Anne realized that Helen would learn more and learn it faster if she had the use of the school's books and facilities. Michael Anagnos, the director of the school, agreed to take Helen as a student at no charge, with Anne to continue teaching her by her own methods, but within the school.

A Schoolgirl Grows Up

Although Helen missed her parents, she was happy at Perkins Institution and her progress was even accelerated. With her beloved "Teacher," as she called Anne, she felt secure and happy. She was taught grammar, arithmetic, and the other subjects that children learn in ordinary schools.

Michael Anagnos was so impressed with Helen's remarkable progress and the miraculous way in which Anne had been able to get through to her that he wrote an article about it for the Perkins annual report. He was enthusiastic in his description of the "miracle" that had taken place. Newspapers soon were notified of this article and they carried stories about the remarkable little girl and her teacher. It was such an inspiring story that just about every newspaper in the United States and England wrote about it. Suddenly Helen and Anne were celebrities.

They received a tremendous amount of mail asking all sorts of curious questions and were constantly asked by the press to answer questions. Anne didn't like this notoriety, for she wanted Helen to continue to develop in as normal an environment as possible.

Many famous people in Boston read about Helen and asked to meet her. Soon she was visiting the poet John Greenleaf Whittier, Dr. Oliver Wendell Holmes, the noted minister Phillips Brooks, and prominent wealthy residents. Helen, though she could have been spoiled by all this attention, re-

---

Helen felt secure and happy at Perkins, though she missed her parents. She was taught grammar, arithmetic, and the other subjects that children learn in ordinary schools. Michael Anagnos (shown with Helen, opposite) was very much impressed with Helen's remarkable progress and wrote an article about her for the Perkins annual report. The story reached the newspapers, and from that time on, both Helen and Anne were celebrities.

mained unselfconscious. She was still an affectionate, impulsive, curious, lively girl.

One day one of Laura Bridgman's former teachers, Mrs. Lamson, came to visit Helen at the school. She had just been on a trip to Norway and she told Helen about it with the manual alphabet. After describing the beautiful scenery, she mentioned that the most important thing she had seen was a blind and deaf Norwegian girl who had learned to speak words.

Helen had never had much hope of learning to speak with her voice, and indeed, it was considered just about impossible. Deaf people were being educated to "read" lips of other people and to form their own lips in the same positions in order to speak the same words. But blind-deaf people could not see other people's lips, and therefore, it was believed, could not learn.

This Norwegian girl, however, had learned to touch people's lips as they were talking. Ragnhild Kaata would touch her own lips and form them in the same positions to speak words. She felt people's throat vibrations, too, and put her hand on her own throat to feel her own vibrations while attempting to speak with her voice. If she could put her lips in the same positions and feel the same throat vibrations, she knew she was speaking the same words.

The moment Helen heard this news, she became very excited about the hopes and possibilities of learning to speak. She was convinced that she could learn if this Norwegian girl had.

Not long afterward, Anne took Helen to an expert, Miss Sarah Fuller, principal of the Horace Mann School for the Deaf in Boston. Miss Fuller knew that Helen faced tremendous obstacles because of her blindness, but she offered to try to teach her to speak.

To everyone's surprise, Helen learned to speak some words very quickly by placing her fingers on Miss Fuller's lips and then having Miss Fuller show her exactly how to form her own lips and tongue. First she learned the vowel sounds, then simple, one-syllable words. Finally, she put words together in her favorite sentence, "I am not dumb now." She spoke this distinctly, and practiced it so she could tell her parents the next time she went home to visit them.

After a series of lessons by Miss Fuller, Anne took over the teaching of voice speech to Helen. At this stage in history, teaching the deaf to speak was still in the experimental stage. Dr. Alexander Graham Bell and other pio-

---

While Helen was at Perkins she met a woman who told her about a young Norwegian girl who was blind and deaf, but who had learned to speak words. Helen was intrigued, and decided that if this girl had learned, so would she. Soon afterward, Anne took Helen to meet Miss Sarah Fuller (opposite). Miss Fuller, who was an expert in teaching the deaf, agreed to try to teach Helen to speak. To everyone's surprise, Helen did learn to speak and be understood.

neers were progressing with good results, but some things were not discovered until years later.

One of these things was that a deaf person who doesn't use his voice suffers from weak vocal cords. Like any muscle that is not used, they get very weak and need a gradual conditioning program to prepare them for use if the person decides to learn to talk. Since this wasn't known when Helen was learning to speak, she injured her vocal cords by trying to speak too much too soon. She tried to speak whole sentences over and over again, and as a result her voice never did have a natural sound because of the injured cords. But she did learn to speak and be understood.

Helen came to love reading books, so much so that she could easily have been content to sit and read for the rest of her life. But Anne would have none of that; she told Helen that she couldn't do much good in the world by being a "bookworm." So, unlike Laura Bridgman, who remained sheltered at the Perkins school practically all her life, Helen Keller went on to a full, active life. She was so energetic and unafraid that she learned to swim, ride horseback, and ride on a tandem bicycle. Anne, of course, stayed at her side, participating with her in all these activities.

Helen blossomed into a girl full of love and compassion. When she heard about a young blind deaf-mute named Tommy Stringer in a poorhouse similar to the one Anne had been in, she was determined to raise money to arrange for him to come to Perkins. Helen's beloved dog, Lioness, had died and newspapers reported it. There were offers of other dogs from all over the world, for people had pity for this brave little girl they had read about. But Helen wrote back to these people in her own pencil-script, asking them instead to send contributions to help poor little Tommy Stringer come to Perkins and be educated. She succeeded in raising enough money through publicity and her personal appeals to rescue

---

Helen is shown here (standing at left) with some of the other students at the Perkins Institution for the Blind. The little boy is Tommy Stringer, who had begun life in a poorhouse similar to the one in which Anne Sullivan had spent her childhood. Helen had heard about Tommy and had succeeded in raising enough money to rescue him. Soon he was a pupil at Perkins, being taught to communicate outside his dark, silent world.

little Tommy. Soon he was a pupil at the school, being helped by Anne and several other teachers to communicate outside his dark, silent world.

Helen's idealistic views of the world received a severe jolt while she was at Perkins. She had met so many influential people, and they had all been so kind to her, that she couldn't imagine the human faults of jealousy and suspicion. She had yet to learn that even basically kind people were capable of these failings.

To please Michael Anagnos, whom she revered, she wrote a fiction story about King Frost, who lived in an ice palace and came to color the leaves with gold in the fall. It was a well-written story for an eleven-year-old, full of imagination and smoothly flowing sentences. Helen was excited about it and read it aloud in her halting voice to her family and Anne during a summer visit to Alabama. She sent it to Mr. Anagnos as a birthday gift.

Mr. Anagnos had done an excellent job of running the Perkins school, following in the footsteps of its founder, Dr. Howe. He knew that institutions such as his needed publicity to attract the attention of influential supporters, and he was intelligent enough to see that Helen was bringing worldwide publicity to the school.

In reports and articles, he extolled the wonders of Helen's ability to learn. He was prone to exaggerate, and he heaped such praise on her accomplishments that she sounded more like a genius than an intelligent, lively girl with human failings. Perkins Institution was mentioned prominently in all these accounts.

A coolness began to develop between Anne and Michael Anagnos. She was indignant with the way his writings painted an unrealistic portrait of Helen and fearful that Helen would soon be smothered in public attention and not allowed to develop normally. His feelings were hurt when Anne had remarked in a newspaper interview that she had sole charge of Helen and was her teacher. It sounded as if Perkins school had played little part in Helen's progress, although Anne hadn't meant it that way. Anagnos had been more than generous, allowing Anne and Helen to use the school's facilities while Anne taught the girl in her own way, outside of classrooms at times.

When Anagnos received Helen's story about frost and the autumn leaves, it was titled "The Frost King" and pub-

---

This photograph of Helen as a calm and lovely young girl, taken when she was a student at Perkins, shows the great change that had taken place in the wild youngster when she had begun to communicate with other people.

lished in the Perkins annual report, to show how well this remarkable girl was doing at Perkins. Little did anyone realize the storm of controversy that it would cause.

Helen didn't realize it until a few months later when Anne told her.

"Helen, someone has written Mr. Anagnos that your story, 'The Frost King' is not your story at all. That it was published long ago in a book, and called 'Frost Fairies.' Think very, very hard. I never read you a story like that. But did anyone else?"

Helen was absolutely sure. "Oh, no, no!" she protested. "I am sure I never heard it. I am perfectly sure I wrote the story myself! Oh, how could there be such a mistake? And now people will think I am untrue and wicked!"

Upon examination, it was discovered that the story was very much like one written years before by Margaret T. Canby in a children's book. Almost sentence for sentence it followed the story line. Yet neither Anne nor any of Helen's relatives could remember reading it to Helen.

Finally, a family friend remembered reading the story to Helen three years previously. The story apparently registered in Helen's subconscious, and with her remarkable memory for detail, came pouring out when she wrote her own story. The famous author Mark Twain remarked that the same thing had happened to him and almost every writer at one time or another.

Michael Anagnos was very upset about the possibility of Helen's plagiarism, and there was some suspicion that Anne had told her what to write in the story or had read the original story to her. He called a "committee of investigation" comprised of four blind teachers and four sighted to "try" Helen and find out the truth.

In her innocence, Helen couldn't imagine why they didn't take her word that she hadn't copied any other story deliberately. The frightened girl was called into a room without Anne and questioned at length by the committee. Some members bluntly accused her of deceiving Mr. Anagnos with the story and lying to get out of it. Eventually four members voted that the child was guilty of stealing the story and four maintained that she was innocent. Anagnos broke the tie by voting that she couldn't have done it deliberately.

It was a shocked, weeping young girl who was finally allowed out of that room. That night she cried for hours, sobbing and protesting her innocence.

"As I lay in my bed that night," she wrote later, "I wept as I hope few children have wept. I felt so cold, I imagined I should die before morning. . . . I think if this sorrow had come to me when I was older, it would have broken my spirit beyond repairing."

Anagnos wrote that he believed Helen innocent of deliberate deceit, but he was very cool toward her and Anne afterward, and Helen could sense this.

"He locked us out of his heart!" she said.

When Mark Twain later heard about the committee "trying" the eleven-year-old girl for plagiarism, he was so furious that he couldn't stop cursing for hours. He referred to the members as "a collection of decayed human turnips."

To please Michael Anagnos, who had been so kind to her, Helen wrote a fiction story as a birthday gift for him. It was a well-written story for an eleven-year-old, and Mr. Anagnos published it in the Perkins annual report to show how well this girl was doing at the school. Months later it was discovered that the story was very much like one that had been published years before in a children's book. Helen was called before a committee of teachers who were to determine whether she had copied the story deliberately. Helen could not understand how they could believe she might do something like that, and it was a shocked and weeping young girl (opposite) who was finally allowed to leave the room.

Mark Tw

Mark Twain, who had been horrified when he heard about the committee "trying" Helen for plagiarism, met her a few years later and began a long, close friendship. They are shown together here in front of a poster announcing one of Mr. Twain's speaking engagements.

Helen continued to have many other influential friends, however, and they were very kind to her. Dr. Alexander Graham Bell invited her to sit with him at the inauguration of President Grover Cleveland in Washington, took her on family picnics, to Niagara Falls, and to the World's Fair in Chicago. Other friends paid her school and living expenses, and Anne's too, when the Keller family finances were shaky.

Through Dr. Bell's influence, it was arranged for Helen to attend the Wright-Humanson Oral School for the Deaf in New York. Here she continued to practice vocal exercises and lip-reading with her fingers. It was hard, slow work and she needed Anne's encouragement to keep her going. Dr. Thomas Humanson, one of the school's founders, personally taught her. He gave her singing lessons as a means of controlling her voice and developing a higher and clearer pitch. She made fairly good progress.

In New York, Helen and Anne met more distinguished friends who admired the courage of both this remarkable girl and her selfless, dedicated teacher. They met Samuel Clemens, or Mark Twain as the famous writer was known, and began a long, close friendship. He grew to love Helen like a daughter and his admiration for Anne's sacrifices and great ability was boundless. Other friends raised money to support both Anne and Helen while Helen went on to school.

By this time she was determined to go to college. Many people were skeptical of her chances to master a college curriculum with her handicaps, but her confidence and enthusiasm were limitless. She could do it, of course, only with "Teacher" sitting at her side, relaying the lectures to her by manual alphabet.

First came nearly four years at the Cambridge School for Young Ladies near Boston, a good college preparatory

school. The lessons were difficult, but with Anne's help Helen managed to keep abreast of the girls in her classes who had normal sight and hearing. Poor Anne's own eyes were so weary from constant reading that doctors were afraid she might lose her sight again, but she refused to give up helping Helen.

At last Helen was graduated and passed the rigid entrance examinations for Radcliffe College. She continued her diligent study habits while at Radcliffe, and her great ability in language showed in her grades in English, German, Latin, and Greek. She not only acquired a good knowledge of English composition, but learned to speak the other languages orally, at least to a limited extent.

It was while she was studying at Radcliffe that she wrote about her life and the miracle of breaking out of her private abyss to communicate with the world. She wrote this in class themes, but soon a national magazine offered her the opportunity to rewrite them into a series of magazine articles. After consulting Anne she agreed, and soon launched into the writing. It proved to be more difficult than she had imagined, with deadlines to meet and still her college work to be done.

When the series appeared in the *Ladies' Home Journal*, it was a national sensation. Her writing was lyrical, imaginative, and she had an inspiring story to tell. A publisher quickly offered to combine them into a book, and Helen agreed to rewrite and expand them.

To help prepare extra material for the book and show her where to edit, the publisher engaged a young Harvard teacher, John Macy. A handsome, personable young man, Macy spent many days going over the manuscript with both Helen and Anne. He became fond of both of them, but especially fond of Anne. Romance blossomed as the book progressed. As soon as the book was published, it became a best seller. Helen Keller became a world-famous author before she graduated from college, and Anne Sullivan's life took a new turn.

Through Dr. Alexander Graham Bell's influence, it was arranged for Helen to attend the Wright-Humanson Oral School for the Deaf in New York. Here she continued to practice vocal exercises and lip-reading with her fingers. Helen became determined to go to college, and after suitable preparation was admitted to Radcliffe College. With Anne Sullivan's help, Helen not only graduated with honors from Radcliffe, but also began to write about her life. It was during this time that Anne (shown at the top of page fifty-eight with Helen) met and fell in love with John Macy, an editor who worked with Helen on her book. Helen, shown in the two photographs at the bottom of page fifty-eight, became a world-famous author before she graduated from college.

Workers For Mankind

In 1905, a year after Helen's graduation from Radcliffe, Anne married John Macy. She had had many doubts before agreeing to marry. For one thing, Macy was several years younger than she; for another, she knew she didn't ever want to abandon Helen to pursue her own separate life.

But John Macy understood her devotion to Helen, and he agreed that the three of them could live together happily. Helen encouraged her to think of her own happiness for once, and Anne finally agreed to marry John. There were difficulties in the marriage as time went by, for Anne's impatient Irish personality often clashed with John's. Neither could escape the limelight as long as Helen lived with them, for as John put it, she was more an institution than a person, as far as the world was concerned. After a few years John left the state to take another job, and the two finally became permanently separated.

Anne and Helen had bought a small house in Wrentham, Massachusetts, after Helen's graduation. This was their home for some time. Helen continued to grow intellectually, reading the classics, history, and philosophy and carrying on correspondence with famous people all over the world. Her book, *The Story of My Life,* was eventually printed in more than fifty languages, and she joined the ranks of people whose names are known in nearly every corner of the globe.

Although the great industrialist Andrew Carnegie had given Helen a pension for life and other friends such

Anne Sullivan and John Macy were married, but the difficulties of living with Helen, who was always in the limelight, eventually led to their separation. Opposite, Helen is shown with Dr. Alexander Graham Bell, a friend who continued to be a guiding influence in her life.

For
The
Blind
Helen Keller

Although many people had helped Helen and Anne financially, they still found it necessary to earn money to live. They gave lectures (left), talking about Helen's education and the opportunities for the blind and deaf. It was about this time that Anne's health began to worry Helen, and the two decided to hire a secretary to accompany them on their tours. They were fortunate in finding a young Scottish girl named Polly Thomson, who immediately became a most important person in their lives.

as the Boston sugar magnate John Spaulding had helped them financially, they still found it necessary to earn money to live. Anne's health was failing and she had to have several operations.

To earn money they embarked on lecture tours, talking about Helen's education and the opportunities for the blind and deaf. In addition to these money-earning ventures, Helen gave much of her time to helping raise money for the blind by appearing at charity affairs. She also spent a large part of her time answering letters from afflicted people all over the world, cheering them and giving them hope.

Anne's health continued to worry Helen. After an incident in a Bath, Maine, hotel when Anne became seriously ill and Helen couldn't grope her way down the stairs to summon help, they decided to hire a secretary to accompany them on lecture tours and live with them. They were fortunate in their choice. She was a young Scottish girl named Polly Thomson who knew nothing about the blind or the deaf, but was a practical person. She was cheerful, a hard worker, and a good manager who took care of running their financial affairs, dealt with callers, and handled the telephone. Anne and Helen quickly learned to love her, and Polly became completely devoted to them.

As Helen wrote later, "Had it not been for her devotion, adaptability, and willingness to give up every individual pleasure, we should long ago have found it necessary to retire into complete isolation."

In Helen's next book, *The World I Live In,* she explained how she used the senses of touch, taste, and smell to substitute for sight and hearing. She told how she could tell by vibration many things that she could not hear, such as the rhythm of music, certain tools being used, and the way different people walked. She realized that people all over the world expected her to be an expert on the problems of the blind, and she studied hard so that she could answer their many letters.

Helen's father had died, and the grief stayed with her for a long time. Her mother began to spend more and more time visiting the house at Wrentham, and later she traveled with Anne, Polly, and Helen on lecture trips. At one point during Anne's illness doctors suspected that she might have tuberculosis and sent her away to a sanitarium for awhile. Polly was taking time off to visit her relatives in Scotland and Helen's mother stayed with her for awhile.

During this time they had hired a young newspaperman to fill in for Polly until she returned. He knew the manual alphabet and could help Helen with her preparation of manuscripts.

Helen was feeling very lonely and sad with Anne and Polly both gone, and the young man comforted her with his kindness. A feeling grew between them as they spent their days together. They talked for long periods with their fingers, and they went for long walks in the autumn woods and fields near the house.

For the first time, Helen was aware of the feeling of romantic love. It was much like those feelings Anne had described to her when she first became attracted to John Macy. It was a new, thrilling experience, and despite her worry over Anne's health, Helen began to find each day exciting and looked forward to the future.

The young man asked her to marry him and refused to listen to her protestations that her handicaps would be a burden. Helen accepted his proposal, but they both agreed to keep silent about it until Anne's health improved and they could tell her and Helen's mother about it.

But they were so eager to make their plans that they applied for a marriage license before telling anyone about it.

At one point during Anne Sullivan's illness, she was sent away to a tuberculosis sanitarium. Polly at the time was on vacation in Scotland, and Helen was very lonely, though her mother was staying with her. They hired a young newspaperman to fill in for Polly, and he and Helen became very close as they spent their days together (opposite). Her mother became very much upset when she discovered that the two young people planned to marry, and sent the young man away. This sad experience haunted Helen for a long time afterward.

A newspaper reporter happened to check the county clerk's register and discovered Helen Keller's name on the list for marriage licenses. The next day the story was in all the papers and Helen's mother read it.

She rushed angrily into Helen's room and asked her in manual language what it was all about. She thought it would be a dreadful mistake for Helen to consider marriage with her handicaps. Helen panicked, not wishing to alarm or hurt her mother, and denied that she was going to be married. Her mother told the young man to go away and never come back. He left, but wrote Helen a braille letter asking her to write to him. They never saw each other again.

The bittersweet experience of unfulfilled love haunted Helen for a long time afterward. After brooding for awhile, she plunged into writing and lecturing again. Anne's health improved after a stay in Puerto Rico, and she, Helen, and Polly were reunited.

During the years 1914-1918, many of the world's leading countries were plunged into the First World War. Germany, Austria, Turkey, and some allied nations were at war against England, France, Russia, and several other countries. It was the first war waged with mechanized equipment. Soldiers moved mostly by troop train and still slogged through mud much of the time, but the British had invented the armored tank to fight on the battlefields, and many supplies were moved by truck. Flimsy airplanes flew overhead and the first aerial combat took place.

After German submarines had sunk American ships in the Atlantic, the United States finally entered the war on the side of England, France, and their allies. A million American soldiers went overseas to thwart the German invasion of France. A young officer named Douglas MacArthur distinguished himself by leading the famed Rainbow Division in combat.

At home, America's industrial might made a big difference in the cause. A seemingly endless supply of weapons, equipment, planes, and ships rolled out of the factories to help the British and

---

Opposite, Helen Keller is shown as she looked during the 1920's.

French troops as well as the Americans. Henry Ford, the brilliant industrialist who had built the giant Ford Motor Company from nothing, put the tremendous ability of his organization behind the effort. Soon Germany acknowledged defeat and an armistice was signed.

During the war Helen devoted a great deal of time and effort to visiting the blinded soldiers in hospitals. She told them that life could go on and that they could still do much good for themselves and others. Helen liked to dance, feeling the vibrations of the music, and she danced with many of the blinded servicemen. Seeing her gave many of them hope at a time when life hardly seemed worth living to them.

In 1918, some of the Hollywood movie moguls suggested to Helen that she play herself in a film of the story of her life. Her lack of a natural-sounding voice wouldn't matter, since movies were silent at that time. Always one to try a new adventure, Helen went to Hollywood and acted in the film. It wasn't a very good movie, though, and it proved a box-office flop.

Next Helen and Anne tried vaudeville performances. The money was good, and Helen won many new friends and helped convince people that the blind and deaf could be educated and accomplish many things if given the chance. Together they told the dramatic story of Helen's life and her rescue from being cut off from the world. The audiences were unfailingly enthusiastic.

After a few years of this, they decided to retire because of the difficulty of performing when Anne's health wasn't good. Polly, Helen, and Anne now lived in a house in Forest Hills, New York. As always in Helen Keller's life, however, she was not content to sit idly by the fire while the rest of the world was in action.

When Anne's health had improved after a stay in Puerto Rico, she, Helen, and Polly were reunited. They continued their lecture tours, and Helen spent much of her time writing. Anne (standing) is shown with Helen in this photograph.

She and Anne soon were deeply involved in the work of a new organization, the American Foundation for the Blind. They worked on campaigns to educate the public about the prevention of blindness. They worked to promote the education and employment of

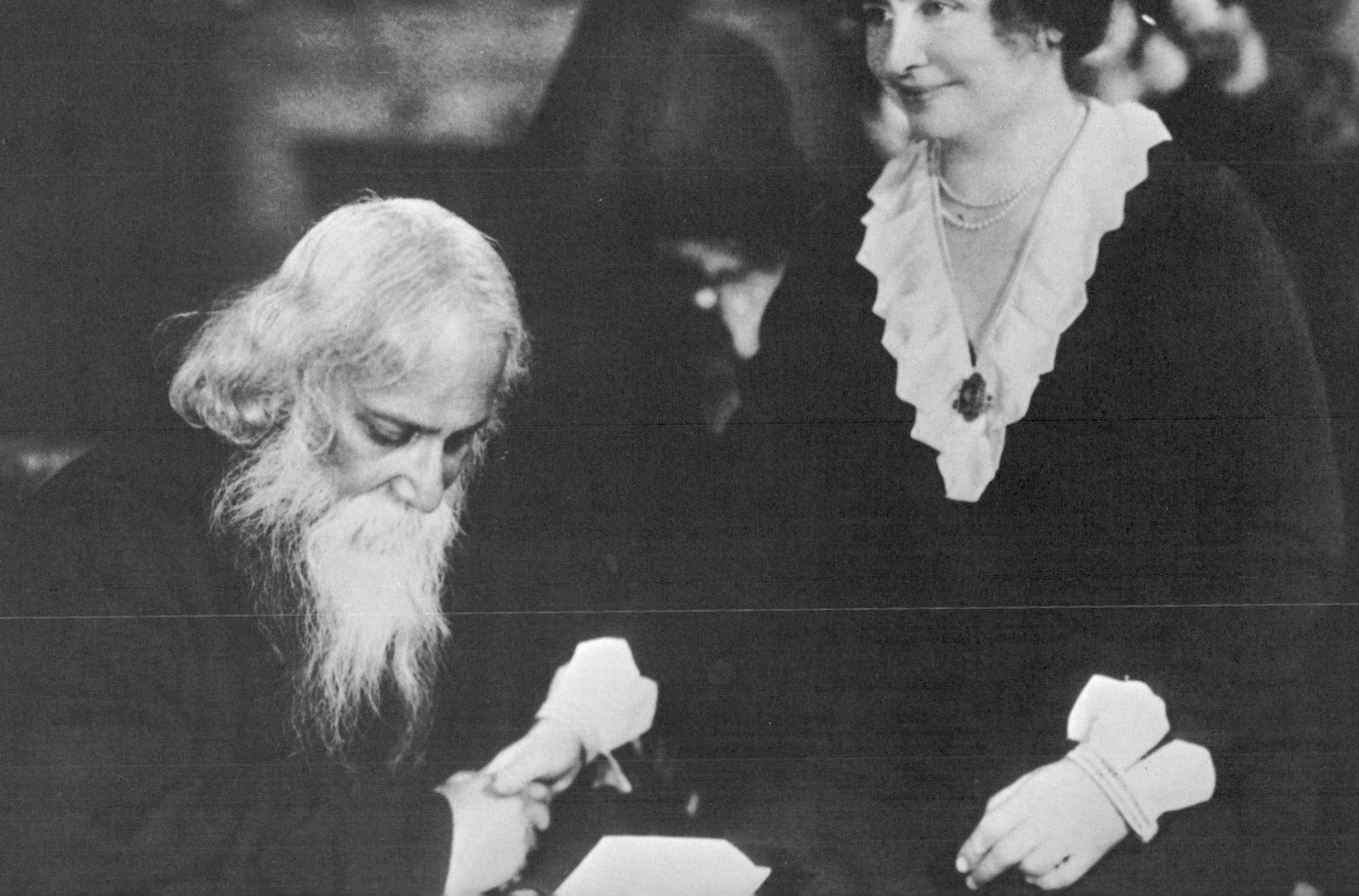

On these pages, Helen is shown with some of the many friends she has made during her life. Opposite, top, with Luther Burbank, the American horticulturist. Opposite, bottom, she is with the Indian poet, Sir Rabindranath Tagore during his visit to the United States in 1930. The year 1926 brought Helen Keller's first friendship with a United States President, Calvin Coolidge, who is shown with her at right. She has known every President since then.

Helen Keller's circle of friends included many famous people from all walks of life. Opposite, top, she is shown with George Bernard Shaw. At the right in the picture is Lady Astor, who introduced Helen to Shaw. Opposite, bottom, Helen is shown in 1931 as she receives the degree of Doctor of Humane Letters from Dr. Charles E. Beury (at left in the picture), President of Temple University. Governor Gifford Pinchot of Pennsylvania, who received the honorary degree of Doctor of Laws, looks on. At right, Helen is shown with Eleanor Roosevelt at a reception honoring Helen in 1936.

blind people. And Helen worked hardest of all to urge the adoption of one standard braille system.

For years there had been problems because five different systems of alphabets for the blind were being used, and they were not compatible. In order to read all books for the blind, it was necessary to know all five systems. Most people had trouble learning even one. Helen had long argued that the system of English braille was the best, and should be used by everyone.

Through her efforts and publicity, the American Foundation for the Blind campaigned for the adoption of this system. In 1932 it became the standard system, and still is. It is almost the exact system that Louis Braille invented in Paris in 1829.

Helen wrote two more books while she was campaigning for the Foundation: *My Religion,* and *Midstream,* the sequel to her first autobiography, *The Story of My Life.* At this point, an author wrote a book about Anne, too, entitled *Anne Sullivan Macy, the Story Behind Helen Keller.* Anne had never spoken of her own tragic childhood until this book was published, and Helen was astonished and touched to realize the difficulties this woman had gone through in her early life. To go through this start in life and still be as selfless and devoted as Anne was seemed beyond the realm of possibility.

The end came at last for Anne in October, 1936, when she was seventy-six years old. She had traveled in Europe with Helen and Polly until the last year of her life. But in that year she lapsed into a coma and died peacefully a few days later with Helen at her side.

One of the world's most noble women was gone. She received more recognition for her part in the miracle of Helen Keller after her death than she had during her life.

Many years before, a newspaper writer had pointed out:

"It is perhaps worth reminding the readers that the wonderful feat of dragging Helen Keller out of her hopeless darkness was only accomplished by sacrificing for it another woman's whole life, and if ever the attempt is made in a similar case, it must be at the same cost."

Anne Sullivan Macy had left some giant footsteps to follow.

In 1936, Anne Sullivan Macy died at the age of seventy-six. She had traveled in Europe with Helen and Polly until the last year of her life, but in that year she lapsed into a coma and died peacefully a few days later. One of the world's most noble women was gone, and a grieving Helen Keller (opposite) was left without her lifelong friend and teacher.

First Lady of Courage

A grieving Helen Keller sailed for Scotland with Polly Thomson after Anne's ashes had been buried at the National Cathedral in Washington, D.C. Polly's brother, a minister in a small Scottish town, had invited the two of them to be with him and his family through the Christmas season and for as long afterward as they wished to stay.

The cheerful Scottish family proved to be a good cure for their grief, and they enjoyed their stay. It was while they were there that they received an invitation from the Japanese government to visit Japan to encourage help for the blind people of that country. Helen quickly agreed, and the following spring she and Polly made the long trip to Japan.

The welcome she received was truly tremendous. It seemed as if everyone in this far-off land had heard of her. Helen held press conferences to state her views on educating the blind and deaf, and she gave talks at schools for the blind and deaf. She met with educational leaders and met the emperor. Helen was the first woman ever allowed to touch the feet of the Great Buddha at the shrine in Nara.

Helen loved everything about Japan —the delightful manners of the people, the customs, the clothes, the food, and

---

After Anne's death, Helen and Polly Thomson went to Scotland to stay with Polly's brother and his family for awhile. While she was there, Helen (in the center of the picture at the bottom of page seventy-seven and Polly at right in the picture) visited a farm in the area. During their visit, the two women received an invitation to visit Japan to encourage help for the blind people of that country. Opposite, top, Helen (in the center) is shown with Prime Minister Hayashi of Japan after her arrival in that country.

In 1937, Polly Thomson (in the center of the picture at the top of page seventy-eight) became an American citizen. Helen Keller (at left in the picture) said at the time: "Now that Miss Thompson has her papers I feel safe. I couldn't carry on without her." The photo at the bottom of page seventy-eight shows Miss Keller at her typewriter in 1941.

the fragrance of the famed Japanese cherry blossoms. Later she visited part of China and Korea before returning home.

The world was taking an ominous turn toward war again as Helen arrived back in the United States. A great financial depression had gripped the countries of Europe as well as America, and ever since 1929, production had been slow and many people could not find jobs. In 1933, Franklin D. Roosevelt had been inaugurated President of the United States. He set vigorous programs in motion to stimulate industrial production and provide more jobs for people. But success had been slow and many people were still depending on relief money and food provided by the government.

In Italy and Germany, fascist leaders had taken over the governments when the people grew impatient with the slow progress of democratic governments. Adolf Hitler, leader of the Nazi Party, became absolute ruler of Germany after he had been in office a short time. He resented the defeat of his country in the First World War and planned to take more territory for Germany, by force if necessary. His government built up a great army and air force, well equipped with the most modern weapons in the world. Benito Mussolini, the dictator in Italy, was his faithful partner in opposing England, France, and the other countries who were alarmed at Germany's rise in strength.

When Hitler demanded some Polish territory and was refused, his armies invaded Poland in September, 1939, and the Second World War began. Great Britain and France quickly came to Poland's defense, but for the first two years the German armies won victory after victory, conquering many European countries.

Meanwhile, in the Orient, military leaders were running Japan. They built that country's industrial ability into a formidable war machine. They wanted to conquer all of the Orient, but the United States threatened to stop them.

On December 7, 1941, Japanese planes attacked the American naval base at Pearl Harbor, Hawaii, and the war in the Pacific began. General Douglas MacArthur earned his place in history with his gallant defense of the Philippines, and later led the American forces to complete victory over Japan. The Japanese government surrendered after the world's first two atomic bombs were dropped on its cities. Douglas MacArthur became Supreme Commander of the Allied Occupation Forces in Japan, and he earned the respect of the Japanese people by reforming their government and governing them in a fair, progressive manner.

Helen Keller again visited thousands of blinded servicemen during the war, talked to them, and gave them hope

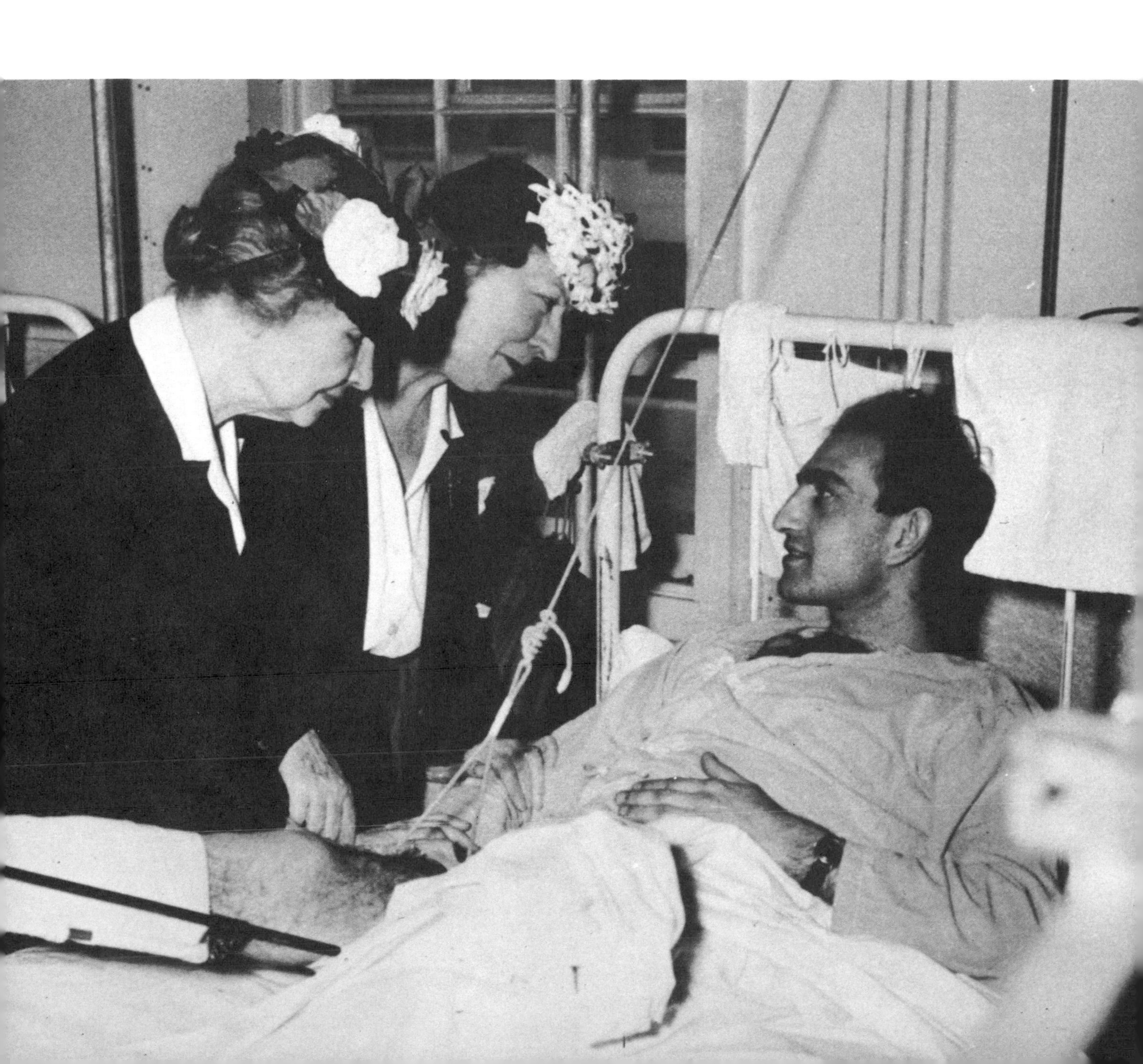

These photographs show Helen Keller during some of her many visits to servicemen in hospitals during World War II. Below left, she and Polly Thomson (center) visit a wounded soldier in a hospital in Georgia. Below, Miss Keller is shown during a visit to hard-of-hearing veterans at a hospital in Santa Barbara, California, as she meets a young man who lost part of his hearing in a South Pacific battle.

846
MP
MP

that they could find pleasure in life despite the loss of their sight. She visited more than seventy hospitals.

Ten years after her visit to Japan she returned, wondering if the people would remember her after the terrible events of the Second World War. This time she had been invited by General MacArthur, who knew that the Japanese people admired her. The reception was even greater this time. The streets of Tokyo were filled as she arrived, and she could feel the outpouring of affection by the people.

One Japanese woman remarked, "For many generations, more than we can count, we bowed our heads and submitted to blindness and beggary. This blind and deaf woman lifts her head high and teaches us to win our way by work and laughter. She brings light and hope to the heart. We Japanese people have need of that."

In the years after the war Helen worked on a book about Anne. When she had it three quarters finished, she took a tour of institutions for the blind in Europe. While she was there, her house burned down with all her belongings, including her manuscript. But as "Teacher" would have wanted her to, Helen started right in again and worked until she had the whole book finished. It was a moving tribute to the courageous Anne, and it was so beautifully written that she would have been very proud of Helen. It was titled simply, *Teacher*. It is one of the most inspiring books ever written.

In 1948, Helen returned to Japan at the invitation of General Douglas MacArthur. Opposite, Miss Keller (center) is escorted to the platform at the Tokyo Bowl where she spoke to thousands of occupation personnel. Her companion, Miss Polly Thomson, is at the right in the picture.

Helen Keller, a trustee of the American Foundation for the Blind, is shown here (second from right) at a 1953 conference of thc organization. Polly Thomson is at the right.

Opposite, Helen Keller is shown on her seventy-fifth birthday. Guiding her hands is Miss Polly Thomson (right). The cake was a gift from the American Foundation for the Blind. In the photograph at right, Miss Keller is shown in 1960 at the dedication of the Anne Sullivan Memorial Fountain at Radcliffe College in Cambridge, Massachusetts. The ceremony symbolized the moment when Helen learned the meaning of her first word, "water," at Tuscumbia, Alabama.

Helen was the guest of honor at a "Helen Keller Luncheon" at Perkins Institution in Boston in 1956, on a very special occasion. It was the dedication of the Keller-Macy Cottage in honor of Helen and Anne, for the purpose of education of the blind-deaf on the spacious campus of the institution. She was pleased to see the expert care and modern methods of teaching at Perkins, especially the use of vibration for the blind-deaf. Instead of the finger alphabet, blind-deaf children are taught right from the start today to read lips and to speak in a clear voice. These methods evolved from the efforts made by Anne and others with Helen. Helen's progress years ago gave educators hope that these new methods would work better.

Today, in her late eighties, Helen Keller lives in Westport, Connecticut, and continues to be one of the most admired people in the world. Polly Thomson has died. Miss Keller continues to be active, and states her views on world events taking place.

This is in keeping with the rest of her life until now. From her early childhood, Helen's curiosity and intelligence foretold that she would never sit on the sidelines if given a chance to play in the game. Anne Sullivan gave her that chance, and the remarkable force and personality of Helen Keller made her a source of inspiration to countless millions in the world. She has been called "the world's First Lady of Courage," and a more fitting name has never been bestowed.

Now in her late eighties, Helen Keller lives in this house in Westport, Connecticut. Though she is no longer active, she continues to be one of the world's most-admired women.

Summary

Helen Keller was not the first deaf, dumb, and blind person in the world to learn to communicate with others. But the little girl from Alabama was destined to accomplish much more than mere communication. She proved that a person without hearing, sight, or the ability to speak can acquire a college education and share in the history, culture, and intellectual life of his country. Even more importantly, she used her ability to communicate by inspiring afflicted people all over the world, in all walks of life. She devoted her life to more than her own education and advancement, and her untiring efforts to help persons with similar handicaps brought widespread results. No longer were these people forced to resign themselves to a dark and limited life, separate from the rest of the world. Helen Keller inspired them to learn as she had learned, and to take an active part in the world as she had done.

The courage that Anne Sullivan had helped Helen develop carried her through many a challenge. She did not rest until improvements in education for the deaf, dumb, and blind had been made, nor until she had helped the world to understand that persons with these handicaps can be helped.

For millions of people Helen Keller stands today as a beacon of hope—a very special woman whose destiny was to show others the way.

Bibliography

"American Mercury Salutes Helen Keller." *American Mercury*, September, 1960.

ANAGNOS, MICHAEL. *Helen Keller*. Reprinted from the Report of the Perkins Institution, Boston, 1892.

BROOKS, VAN WYCK. *Helen Keller; Sketch for a Portrait*. New York: Dutton, 1956.

"Distinguished Lady—Portrait of Helen Keller." *Newsweek*, March 26, 1956.

DUFFUS, P. L. "At Eighty, The Miracle of Helen Keller." *New York Times Magazine*, June 26, 1960.

FARIS, JOHN T. *Men Who Conquered*. Chicago: 1922.

FENNER, M. S. "Editors Notebook." *NEA Journal*, November, 1963.

"Gallant Lady Meets Herself When Young." *Life*, March 30, 1962.

GIBSON, WILLIAM. *The Miracle Worker*. New York: Knopf, 1957.

"Good Companion—Helen Keller." *Life*, April 4, 1960.

"Great Photo Tells A Moving Story—Helen Keller's fingers see the President's smile." *Life*, November 16, 1953.

HARRITY, RICHARD and RALPH G. MARTIN. *The Three Lives of Helen Keller*. New York: Doubleday, 1962.

"Helen Keller—Portrait." *Newsweek*, July 8, 1957.

"Helen Keller—Portrait." *Time*, November 16, 1953.

"Helen Keller—Portrait." *Newsweek*, November 18, 1953.

"Helen Keller—Unconquered." *Time*, July 12, 1954.

HENNY, NELLA BRADDY. "Helen Keller." *New York Times Magazine*, June 26, 1955.

———. *Anne Sullivan Macy, The Story Behind Helen Keller*. New York: Doubleday, 1933.

HICKOK, L. A. *The Touch of Magic*. New York: Dodd, Mead, 1961.

HOWE, MAUD and FLORENCE HOWE HALL. *Laura Bridgman*. Boston: 1903.

KELLER, HELEN. *The Story of My Life*. New York: Doubleday, 1954.

———. *Midstream, my later life*. New York: Doubleday, 1930.

———. *Teacher, Anne Sullivan Macy*. New York: Doubleday, 1957.

———. *Helen Keller's Journal*. New York: Doubleday, 1938.

———. *Optimism, An Essay*. New York: Cromwell, 1903.

———. *The Open Door*. New York: Doubleday, 1957.

———. *The World I Live In*. New York: Century, 1908.

———. *My Religion*. New York: Citadel Press, 1963.

Helen Keller Souvenirs, First & Second Editions, Volta Bureau, Washington, D.C., 1892-1899.

LAMSON, MARY S. *Life and Education of Laura Bridgman*, 1878.

MAETERLINCK, GEORGETTE. *The Girl Who Found The Bluebird*. 1914.

"Negro Leaders Hail Helen Keller." *Negro History Bulletin*, March, 1955.

Reports of the Perkins Institution for 1886, 1887, 1888, 1892.

RICHARDS, LAURA E. *The Story of an Opened Door*. 1928.

RICHARDS, LAURA, ed. *The Life and Letters of Louis Howe*. Boston: 1910.

ROGOW, L. "Miss Keller For Posterity." *Saturday Review*, June 12, 1954.

"Story of Helen Keller." *Life*, June 21, 1954.

SMITH, B. "Walk With Helen Keller." *Cosmopolitan*, December, 1954.

WAITE, HELEN. *Valiant Companions. Helen Keller and Anne Sullivan Macy*. Philadelphia: Macrae Smith Co., 1959.

Index

Acknowledgments: Photographs on pages 2-3, 8, 13 (top), 45, 61, 67, 68, 70, 71, 72, 73, 77, 78, 80, 81, 82, 84-85, 86, 87, and 88-89 from the files of Wide World Photos, Inc.; photographs on pages 11, 13 (bottom), 52, 58, and 91 courtesy of the Helen Keller Property Board, Tuscumbia, Alabama; photographs on pages 47 and 51 courtesy of the Perkins School for the Blind. Illustrations on pages 15, 17, 18, 21, 22, 24, 27, 29, 30, 33, 35, 36, 39, 41, 43, 48, 54, 57, 62, 65, 75, and 83 by John Downs, Hollis Associates.